CHILDREN'S STORYTELLERS

J.K. Rowling

by Chris Bowman

BLASTOFF! READERS
4

BELLWETHER MEDIA • MINNEAPOLIS, MN

Note to Librarians, Teachers, and Parents:

Blastoff! Readers are carefully developed by literacy experts and combine standards-based content with developmentally appropriate text.

Level 1 provides the most support through repetition of high-frequency words, light text, predictable sentence patterns, and strong visual support.

Level 2 offers early readers a bit more challenge through varied simple sentences, increased text load, and less repetition of high-frequency words.

Level 3 advances early-fluent readers toward fluency through increased text and concept load, less reliance on visuals, longer sentences, and more literary language.

Level 4 builds reading stamina by providing more text per page, increased use of punctuation, greater variation in sentence patterns, and increasingly challenging vocabulary.

Level 5 encourages children to move from "learning to read" to "reading to learn" by providing even more text, varied writing styles, and less familiar topics.

Whichever book is right for your reader, Blastoff! Readers are the perfect books to build confidence and encourage a love of reading that will last a lifetime!

This edition first published in 2016 by Bellwether Media, Inc.

No part of this publication may be reproduced in whole or in part without written permission of the publisher. For information regarding permission, write to Bellwether Media, Inc., Attention: Permissions Department, 5357 Penn Avenue South, Minneapolis, MN 55419.

Library of Congress Cataloging-in-Publication Data

Bowman, Chris, 1990-
  J.K. Rowling / by Chris Bowman.
    pages cm. – (Blastoff! Readers: Children's Storytellers)
  Summary: "Simple text and full-color photographs introduce readers to J.K. Rowling. Developed by literacy experts for students in kindergarten through third grade"– Provided by publisher.
  Includes bibliographical references and index.
  Audience: Ages 5-8
  Audience: K to grade 3
  ISBN 978-1-62617-266-1 (hardcover: alk. paper)
  1. Rowling, J. K. 2. Authors, English–20th century–Biography. 3. Potter, Harry (Fictitious character) 4. Children's stories–Authorship. I. Title.
  PR6068.O93Z5547 2016
  823'.914–dc23
  [B]
                          2015004227

Printed in the United States of America, North Mankato, MN.

Table of Contents

J.K. Rowling is the **pen name** of award-winning author Joanne Rowling. She created Harry Potter and his world.

fun fact

J.K. stands for Joanne Kathleen. This is a combination of her and her grandmother's names.

The book **series** is a hit with readers everywhere. Since 1997, more than 450 million copies of her **novels** have been sold!

The Girl Who Dreamed

Jo Rowling was born on July 31, 1965, in Yate, England. She lived with her parents and younger sister, Dianne.

"Read anything you can get your hands on."
J.K. Rowling

Yate, England

As a young girl, Jo liked to read and write. She and Dianne often made up stories together. They acted these stories out with other kids in the neighborhood.

Jo worked hard at her studies. She was voted **head girl** in her last year at school. She did especially well in English and French.

In college, Jo studied French. She planned to become a **secretary**. But she still dreamed of a writing **career**.

"**Differences of habit and language are nothing at all if our aims are identical and our hearts are open.**"
—*Harry Potter and the Goblet of Fire*

Jo worked as a secretary after she graduated in 1986. In her free time, she continued creating stories.

"**We do not need magic to change the world, we carry all the power we need inside ourselves already: we have the power to imagine better.**"

–Harry Potter and the Sorcerer's Stone

fun fact

Jo first thought up the Harry Potter series in 1990. She was riding a train from Manchester to London.

By 1991, she needed a change. Jo moved to Portugal to teach English. While there, she fell in love. She soon got married, and in 1993, gave birth to a daughter.

Unfortunately, Jo's marriage was short-lived. She was unhappy with her husband. Jo decided to move to Edinburgh, Scotland. She and her daughter would be closer to Dianne.

Jo had little money. It was tough to find work as a single mother. She got **assistance** from the government. A **loan** helped her go to school to become a teacher. In her free time, she worked on her book about a boy wizard.

"It is our choices...
that show what we
truly are, far more
than our abilities."
—Harry Potter and the
Chamber of Secrets

By late 1995, Jo finished the first **draft** of *Harry Potter and the Sorcerer's Stone*. She found an **agent** who sent her story to **publishers**. The first 12 publishers **rejected** Jo. But the thirteenth said yes.

Uncorrected Proof Copy

J.K. Rowling

Harry Potter and the Philosopher's Stone

BLOOMSB

! fun fact

An American publisher paid $105,000 to print the Harry Potter books. This is a record for a first-time children's writer!

SELECTED WORKS

Harry Potter and the Sorcerer's Stone (1997)

Harry Potter and the Chamber of Secrets (1998)

Harry Potter and the Prisoner of Azkaban (1999)

Harry Potter and the Goblet of Fire (2000)

Fantastic Beasts and Where to Find Them (2001)

Quidditch Through the Ages (2001)

Harry Potter and the Order of the Phoenix (2003)

Harry Potter and the Half-Blood Prince (2005)

Harry Potter and the Deathly Hallows (2007)

The Tales of Beedle the Bard (2008)

In 1997, her book became an immediate success. Pottermania had begun!

Jo wrote six more novels after the *Sorcerer's Stone* to complete the Harry Potter series. The books follow a boy wizard named Harry as he goes through magic school, faces evil wizards, and deals with growing up.

Jo's books cover many **themes**. Her characters often struggle with the choices they make. Many of them choose to be good. But sometimes even the best wizards make bad decisions.

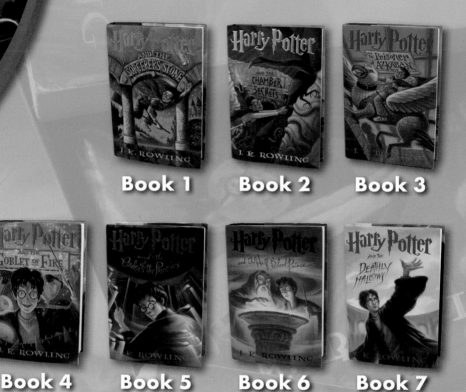

Book 1   Book 2   Book 3

Book 4   Book 5   Book 6   Book 7

"It does not do to dwell on dreams and forget to live."
–Harry Potter and the Sorcerer's Stone

Jo also writes about the importance of friendship. Throughout the stories, Harry is brave and skilled. But he would not succeed without the help of his friends.

Her novels also teach **tolerance**. Some wizards in her books look down on people who do not have magic. However, one of Harry's best friends is from a non-magic family. Jo shows that her background does not affect her magical abilities.

POP CULTURE CONNECTION

The Wizarding World of Harry Potter opened at the Universal Studios Florida theme park in 2010. Guests can shop in Diagon Alley, explore Hogsmeade, and even break into Gringotts Bank!

Harry Potter has **inspired** millions of kids to read. Jo does not currently plan to write any more Harry Potter books. But she has released some short stories about his world.

IMPORTANT DATES

1965: Jo Rowling is born on July 31.

1990: The idea for the Harry Potter books comes to Jo while she is riding a train.

1995: Jo finishes the first draft of *Harry Potter and the Sorcerer's Stone.*

1997: The British Book Awards names *Harry Potter and the Sorcerer's Stone* the Children's Book of the Year.

1998: *Harry Potter and the Chamber of Secrets* wins Children's Book of the Year at the British Book Awards.

2001: Jo is awarded the Order of the British Empire.

2004: The WH Smith Fiction Award is given to Jo.

2008: Jo receives a Lifetime Achievement Award at the British Book Awards.

Order of the British Empire award

2010: The Hans Christian Andersen Literature Award is presented to Jo.

2012: Jo's first book for adults, *The Casual Vacancy,* is released.

She has also written books for adults. She continues to cast a spell on readers of all ages.

Glossary

agent—someone who helps an author get published

assistance—money and food from a government program to help people with little money

career—a job someone does for a long time

draft—a version of something made before the final version

head girl—the girl chosen to represent her school and help younger students

inspired—gave someone an idea about what to do or create

loan—money that is borrowed

novels—longer written stories, usually about made-up characters and events

pen name—a name used by a writer instead of the writer's real name

publishers—companies that make and print books

rejected—turned down

secretary—a person who makes appointments and keeps records for an office

series—a number of things that are connected in a certain order

themes—important ideas or messages

tolerance—keeping an open mind about people from other backgrounds

To Learn More

AT THE LIBRARY

Fraser, Lindsey. *Conversations with J.K. Rowling.* New York, N.Y.: Scholastic, 2001.

Pezzi, Bryan. *J.K. Rowling.* New York, N.Y.: AV2 by Weigl, 2013.

Rowling, J.K. *Harry Potter and the Sorcerer's Stone.* New York, N.Y.: A.A. Levine Books, 1998.

ON THE WEB

Learning more about J.K. Rowling is as easy as 1, 2, 3.

1. Go to www.factsurfer.com.

2. Enter "J.K. Rowling" into the search box.

3. Click the "Surf" button and you will see a list of related web sites.

With factsurfer.com, finding more information is just a click away.

Index

The images in this book are reproduced through the courtesy of: Suzanne Plunkett/ Corbis, front cover, p. 20; Frances M. Roberts/ Newscom, front cover (illustration, background), p. 14 (right); Bellwether Media, all interior backgrounds, pp. 9, 10, 15 (right), 17 (books); Carlo Allegri/ Corbis, p. 4; James Leynse/ Corbis, pp. 4-5; Alpha/ Zuma Press, p. 7; RexUSA, pp. 8-9; Mike Floyd/ Daily Mail/ RexUSA, pp. 10-11; Carolyn Franks, p. 12; Sion Touhig/ Corbis, pp. 12-13; Stephen Butler/ RexUSA, p. 14 (left); Handout/ KRT/ Newscom, p. 15 (left, middle); PR Newswire/ AP Images, pp. 16-17, 19 (right); Mehdi Taamallah/ ABACA/ Newscom, p. 18; Stephen Searle/ Alamy, p. 19 (left); Reuters/ Corbis, p. 21.